Quin was a friendly que
lived in a large rainfores
beak, colourful green fe
red feathered belly brightened up any
part of the rainforest.

It used to be very beautiful in the lush tropical woods with many different kinds of trees, flowers and plenty of fruit. Before, you could hear the loud tweeting of birds and the rustling sounds of wildlife moving around.

Now it was much quieter and not as pretty. Quin and other quetzalla's wanted to find a new home because the rainforest was being destroyed and they did not feel safe in it anymore. People cut trees down, quetzalla's were stolen, and there was horrible smoke in the air.

There was a story an old, wise quetzalla bird told to little hatchlings about a beautiful, magical land called Quetzalla Land. In the story, there is a secret entrance that is very hard to find, and only a special key can open it.

Through the door is a magical land where quetzalla's are safe and wishes and dreams come true. Fairies, giant butterflies, plenty of trees with tasty fruit are some of the things found in this land. Every quetzalla is given a tree home with a magic bell which brings them anything that they want! The birds believed that this land was real, and they wanted to find it.

Quin needed the help of other quetzalla's to discover Quetzalla Land, so he joined a group of them to look for it. They flew between the trees of the rainforest day after day, searching for the entrance. One day, while they were still searching for the secret door, Quin, caught sight of some delicious looking avocados, so he swooped down to one of the trees and landed by the fruit to have a snack.

After Quin finished eating a piece of avocado, he tried to catch up with the other quetzalla's, but he could not find them.

For a long time, Quin searched for the other birds and the secret entrance. Just when he started to give up, he noticed a brightly glowing area of a tree trunk. As Quin moved closer, he saw a red squirrel who was sitting on a branch next to a large glowing key. The key had shape outlines on it.

"You have found the entrance to secret Quetzalla Land. I've noticed you flying around looking sad, and I want to help you. I have seen a lot of quetzalla birds open and enter the invisible door on this tree. If you find the missing parts of the key, it will unlock and open the secret door.

2D shapes are flat shapes. They are the missing parts and what you need to find to make the key work. 2D is short for two-dimensional and you must look for flat shapes. Please be quick because the key to the entrance changes every day!" said the squirrel. Then he pointed to each shape and said, "You need to find a circle, triangle, square, rectangle, pentagon and hexagon."

Quickly, Quin flapped his wings extra fast while flying to a nearby village. Humans had made a lot of buildings, and he saw shapes in many places around the area.

First, Quin saw a square window on a house, then he saw a rectangle door, and after that, a oval hole in a fence. There was a circle on the house, and a star was on top of a tree. Shapes were all around him, but he could not take them with him to the magical land as they were too big.

Soon, Quin caught whiffs of something delicious coming from outside one of the houses, so he followed the scent. A little girl was cooking some tasty looking star-shaped biscuits!

As soon as he landed by her, she said, "Hello, I'm Luna". This little girl was different from other humans because she could speak to and understand animals. They chatted for a while, and Quin told her about the key and the shapes he needed. Suddenly, Quin had an idea to make more shape biscuits, so he asked Luna for help.

She knew how many corners and sides the different shapes had. Luna also knew how to measure and she was happy to help him. They made the shapes by rolling out the dough, carefully measuring lengths and then cutting.

Quin wanted to make sure that he had the correct number of sides and corners for each shape. "A corner is where two sides meet. A side is the straight line between the two corners of a shape. Let's count carefully together as we touch the sides and corners of shape while counting," Luna said.

First, they made a circle which had a continuous curved line. It had no corners.

circle

After, they made a triangle and counted three corners and three sides.

1, 2, 3

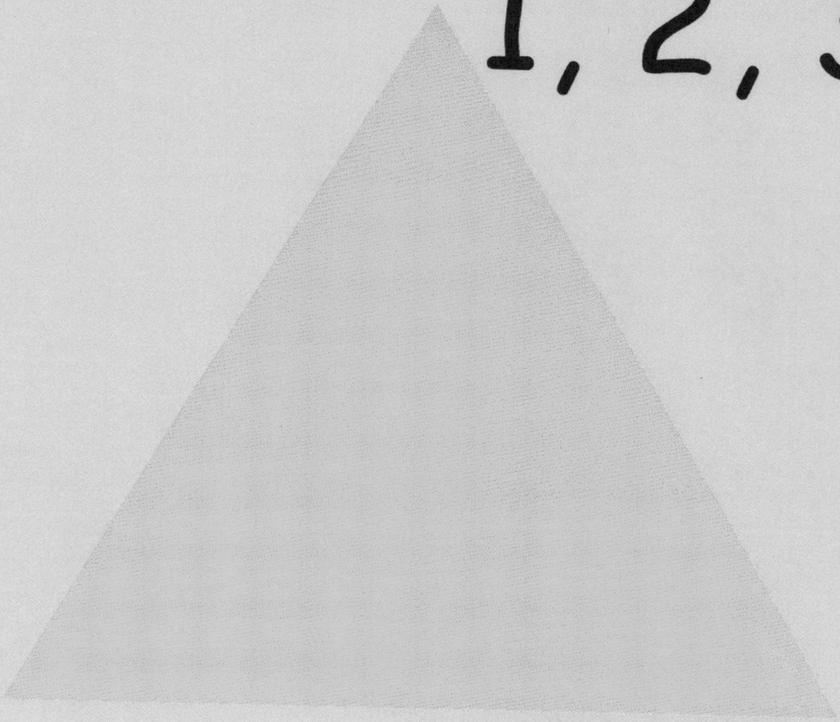

triangle

Next a square with four corners and four sides.

square

Then a rectangle with four corners and four sides. Sometimes this shape is also called an oblong.

rectangle
/oblong

After that, a pentagon with five corners and five sides.

pentagon

Finally, a hexagon with six corners and six sides.

hexagon

When Quin finished making the shapes, he thanked Luna and then flew as fast as he could back to the tree with the key.

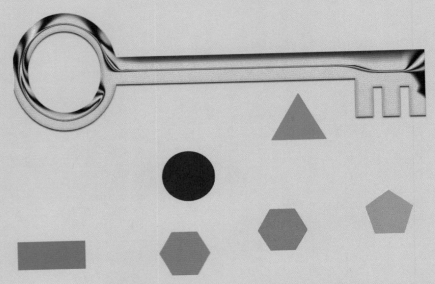

He carefully placed each shape in its area on the key.

Suddenly, the light turned to a brighter colour and other shapes appeared. A door then opened on the tree!

Quin flew through the door with great excitement. As he hovered in the air, Quin saw bright colours, plenty of fruit, and beautiful rainbows with fairies fluttering near them. The other quetzalla birds were flying around happily or resting in their home with a magic bell!

He found a beautiful tree and he lived joyfully in Quetzalla Land with the other birds.

There were hardly any quetzalla birds left in the rainforest where Quin used to live. People missed seeing the beautiful birds, so they started to think more about how they could make them come back. They began producing less smoke, fewer trees were cut down, and great effort was made to keep all kinds of animals safe.

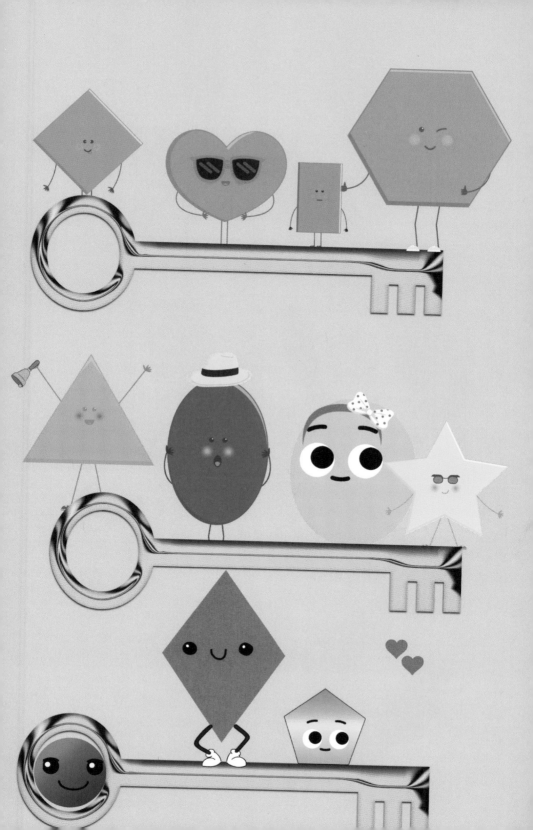

Printed in Great Britain
by Amazon

25309691R00016